GUADELOUPE

TRAVEL GUIDE

2024

FIONA S. WOODWARD

Copyright Page

Table of Contents

Introduction

Welcome to Guadeloupe

Guadeloupe isn't your typical Caribbean island. Sure, it boasts swaying palm trees, translucent turquoise waters, and beaches that gleam like crushed pearls. But beneath that postcard-perfect veneer lies a unique blend of French influence and vibrant Creole culture, making it a destination that tantalizes all your senses.

Imagine this: You wander through a bustling marketplace in Pointe-à-Pitre, the air thick with the aroma of freshly baked baguettes mingling with the sweet scent of exotic fruits. You snag a steaming cup of strong coffee, then weave your way past stalls overflowing with colorful madras fabric and hand-carved wooden sculptures. The melodic lilt of French mingles with the rhythmic chatter of Creole, creating a symphony all its own.

Guadeloupe is a land of two distinct personalities. Grande-Terre, the eastern island, offers a taste of the French Riviera in the Caribbean. Here, you'll find chic resorts lining sugar-white beaches, casinos pulsating with energy and charming cafes spilling out onto cobblestone streets.

But just a short ferry ride away lies Basse-Terre, a nature lover's paradise. This lush, mountainous island is dominated by the still-smoldering peaks of La Soufrière volcano. Hike through emerald rainforests teeming with exotic birds, chase cascading waterfalls that plunge into crystal-clear pools, or soak up the panoramic views from volcanic craters.

Guadeloupe isn't just about the sights; it's about the experiences. You can learn the secrets of Creole cuisine from a local chef, kayak through vibrant coral reefs teeming with colorful fish, or sway to the pulsating rhythms of Gwo ka music under a star-studded sky. Whether you crave relaxation on a pristine beach or adventure in the wild heart of the island, Guadeloupe has something to stir your soul.

So, pack your bags, embrace the spirit of discovery, and get ready to be captivated by the unique charm of this unforgettable Caribbean island.

Geography and Location

Guadeloupe isn't your average Caribbean island. Instead of a single landmass, it's a stunning archipelago, a butterfly-shaped splatter of islands dancing on the turquoise waters where the northeastern Caribbean Sea meets the Atlantic Ocean.

The two main islands, Basse-Terre and Grande-Terre, are the stars of the show. Basse-Terre, the wilder western wing, is a mountainous marvel. Lush rainforests cloak its volcanic peaks, with the still-active Soufrière volcano the undisputed champion, reaching for the sky at a staggering 1467 meters. Think dramatic waterfalls cascading down verdant slopes, hidden black sand beaches whispering secrets, and steaming fumaroles hinting at the fiery heart beneath.

Grande-Terre, the eastern counterpart, is a flatter island, a playground of limestone bathed in golden sunshine. Picture swaying sugar cane fields rippling in the breeze, pristine white sand beaches perfect for sunbathing, and calm turquoise lagoons that beckon you to snorkel through vibrant coral reefs.

This isn't the whole story, though. Guadeloupe's charm extends beyond these two main islands. Marie-Galante, the "Island of a Hundred Windmills," is a laid-back gem known for its rolling hills and friendly locals. La Désirade, a smaller, desert-like island, offers a stark contrast with its rugged beauty and secluded coves. And don't forget Les Saintes, a picture-perfect archipelago south of Basse-Terre, with its charming villages and idyllic bays.

Guadeloupe's location places it right in the sweet spot of the Caribbean. Being part of the Leeward Islands in the Lesser Antilles chain means it enjoys a delightful tropical climate year-round, tempered by cool trade winds. To the north, you'll find Antigua and Barbuda, while Dominica lies to the south. Martinique, another French Caribbean gem, is just a short hop to the south as well.

So, Guadeloupe's not just a beautiful island, it's a gateway to exploring the wider magic of the Caribbean. From volcanic peaks to coral reefs, Guadeloupe's diverse geography offers something for every adventurer.

Climate and Weather

Guadeloupe's weather is like a good friend – reliable, warm, and always ready for a little fun. Here, you can ditch the heavy winter coats and embrace sunshine-filled days almost year-round.

Think of it as having two sides to the coin. The dry season, stretching from December to April, is the golden child. Sunsets paint the sky in fiery hues, and gentle trade winds keep things comfortably cool. This is the prime time for beach bums, with calm seas perfect for swimming and snorkeling. Rainfall is minimal, so pack your swimsuit and get ready for long, sunny days.

But don't underestimate the wet season, from May to November. Yes, there's a chance of afternoon showers, but they tend to be quick bursts that clear the skies even faster. Lush greenery explodes after a rain shower, and the island takes on an almost magical emerald glow. Plus, the crowds thin out a bit, and you might even snag some off-season deals.

Here's a heads-up: Hurricane season officially runs from June to November, but the peak risk is typically from August to October. Don't let that deter you completely – Guadeloupe is well-prepared for these storms, and most of the time, they pass by without causing major disruptions. Just be sure to stay informed about weather forecasts before your trip.

No matter when you visit, Guadeloupe's tropical climate ensures warm temperatures. Expect highs to hover around 27°C (81°F) year-round, with nights dipping down to a pleasant 21°C (70°F). The water temperature follows suit, making it perfect for swimming or trying your hand at water sports any time of year.

So, pack for sunshine, but don't forget a light rain jacket in case an afternoon shower decides to join the party.

Guadeloupe's weather is all about embracing the unexpected and enjoying the island's beauty in all its forms.

Culture and Languages

Guadeloupe's culture is a simmering pot of influences, a rich gumbo flavored by its unique history. The main ingredients? A generous helping of French heritage, a dash of African traditions, a sprinkle of Amerindian customs, and a whole lot of Caribbean spirit. This unique blend makes Guadeloupe a place where baguettes share shelf space with colorful madras fabric, and the melodic lilt of French mingles with the rhythmic beat of Gwo ka music.

French is the official language, a legacy of the island's colonial past. But the heart and soul of Guadeloupe lies in Creole, a language born from the melting pot of cultures. Imagine a vibrant mix of French vocabulary, African rhythms, and a dash of Amerindian thrown in for good measure. While Creole isn't widely spoken in official settings, you'll hear it on the streets, in markets, and from friendly locals. It's a window into the island's soul, a reminder of its rich heritage.

Culture is more than just language, though. Guadeloupe's spirit comes alive in its traditions. Immerse yourself in the vibrant energy of a Gwo ka music performance, where powerful drumbeats and rhythmic chants transport you to another world. Wander through a bustling market, your senses overwhelmed by the intoxicating aroma of spices and the sight of colorful fabrics. Don't be surprised if you're invited to a lively street party, fueled by infectious music and overflowing with delicious Creole cuisine.

Religion also plays a significant role in Guadeloupean life. The majority of the population is Roman Catholic, with a strong influence on African traditions. This unique blend is evident in festivals like Saint-Jacques Day, where colorful boat processions pay homage to the patron saint of fishermen.

Guadeloupe's cultural scene thrives on its artistic spirit. Explore local galleries brimming with vibrant paintings and intricate sculptures that capture the essence of the island. Literature lovers can delve into the works of local authors who weave tales steeped in history and Creole traditions.

So, Guadeloupe's culture isn't just something you observe – it's something you experience. Embrace the warmth of the people, immerse yourself in the rhythmic pulse of the music, and savor the delicious flavors of the cuisine. Guadeloupe's cultural gumbo is waiting to be explored, and it's sure to leave you with a taste you won't soon forget.

CHAPTER 1. Planning Your Trip

Guadeloupe, a butterfly-shaped archipelago in the Caribbean, beckons with volcanic peaks, turquoise coves, and swaying palm trees. But before you pack your swimsuit and sunscreen, there's the key question: when is the best time to visit? Here's a breakdown of Guadeloupe's seasons to help you pick the perfect time for your island adventure.

Best Time to Visit

Sun-Kissed Shores and Clear Skies: The Dry Season (December-April)

This is the peak tourist season for a reason. With blissful sunshine, pleasantly warm temperatures averaging around 27°C (80°F), and calm seas, it's ideal for beach bums and water babies. Hike the lush trails of Basse-Terre National Park, snorkel the vibrant coral reefs teeming with colorful fish, or simply relax on the sugar-white sands of Grande-Terre.

Pros: Perfect weather for outdoor activities, calm seas for diving and snorkeling, and lively atmosphere with festivals and cultural events.

Cons: Higher prices for flights and accommodation, larger crowds at popular spots.

Shoulder Seasons: Finding the Sweet Spot (May-June & November)

If you're looking for a balance between good weather and budget-friendly travel, consider the shoulder seasons. May and June see the tail-end of the dry season, with occasional showers that keep things green and lush, and slightly lower prices. Similarly, November offers a taste of the dry season with sunny days and the start of festive holiday decorations.

Pros: Generally good weather with fewer crowds, potentially lower travel costs.

Cons: A slightly higher chance of rain showers, so some water activities might be affected.

Embrace the Green: The Wet Season (July-October)

Guadeloupe transforms during the wet season. Lush rainforests come alive, waterfalls cascade down mountainsides, and the island explodes with vibrant greenery. While there are more frequent rain showers, they tend to be brief and refreshing, followed by bursts of sunshine. This is a fantastic time for nature enthusiasts and those seeking a more secluded escape.

Pros: The most affordable travel options, fewer crowds, breathtakingly lush landscapes.

Cons: Increased chance of rain showers, some water activities might be affected, potential for rougher seas.

Hurricane Season: A Note of Caution (Mid-August to Late October)

The official hurricane season runs from mid-August to late October. While Guadeloupe isn't directly hit as often as some islands, it's best to avoid this period altogether if you're set on a worry-free vacation.

Festival Fever: Plan Your Trip Around the Fun

Guadeloupe bursts with cultural celebrations throughout the year. Time your trip for the vibrant Carnival in February and March, or immerse yourself in the Gwoka music festival in July. Researching upcoming events can add an extra layer of excitement to your Guadeloupe adventure.

Remember: This is just a guide. Guadeloupe's charm lies in its year-round beauty. So, consider what kind of experience you crave - sun-soaked relaxation, budget-conscious exploration, or a taste of the island's vibrant culture - and pick the season that best suits your travel dreams.

Entry Requirements and Visa Information

Guadeloupe, a French Caribbean gem, awaits with open arms (and some formalities). Before you jet off to this paradise, brushing up on entry requirements and visa information will ensure a smooth arrival.

Do You Need a Visa? It Depends...

Guadeloupe follows French visa regulations. The good news is that many nationalities can enter visa-free for stays up to 90 days, provided it's for tourism or business visits.

The Visa-Free List: Are You On It?

Citizens of the European Union, Switzerland, Iceland, Norway, and most countries in North and South America (including the US and Canada) can generally waltz through immigration without a visa. However, it's always wise to double-check with a French embassy or consulate in your home country. They'll confirm if you fall under the visa-free umbrella and can advise on any specific documentation needed.

Beyond 90 Days? Gear Up for a Visa Application

If your Guadeloupean adventure stretches beyond 90 days, or you're planning to work or study on the island, you'll need to apply for a visa. The type of visa required depends on your purpose of stay. Contact the French embassy or consulate for details on specific visa categories, application procedures, and any fees involved.

Passport Power: Your Ticket to Paradise

No matter your visa situation, a valid passport is your golden ticket to Guadeloupe. Ensure your passport has at least 6 months of validity remaining from your planned departure date. Having a few blank pages for entry and exit stamps is also a good idea.

Packing Tips

Packing the Essentials: Beyond Swimwear

Here are some additional documents that immigration officials might request upon arrival:

Proof of Onward Travel: This could be a return flight ticket or a confirmation for onward travel to another destination.

Accommodation Details: Show them your hotel reservation or confirmation of your holiday rental.

Proof of Sufficient Funds: This demonstrates you have enough money to support yourself during your stay. The exact amount can vary, so check with the French authorities for current guidelines.

Embassy All-Stars: Your Visa Application Allies

The French embassy or consulate in your home country is your best resource for navigating visa applications. They can provide specific requirements, and application forms, and answer any questions you might have. Some embassies allow online applications, while others require in-person visits.

Entering with Ease: A Breeze Through Immigration

Upon arrival in Guadeloupe, head to the immigration control area. Have your passport, visa (if required), and any requested documentation readily available. The immigration officer will review your paperwork and ask a few questions about your trip.

Voila! You're In!

With a smile and a "Bienvenue en Guadeloupe" (welcome to Guadeloupe!), you'll be cleared to enter this captivating island paradise. Now, the real adventure begins!

Getting There and Getting Around

Guadeloupe beckons with its volcanic peaks, turquoise waters, and laid-back charm. But before you start picturing yourself sipping cocktails on a beach lounger, there's the matter of transportation. Here's your roadmap to navigating your Guadeloupe getaway, from touchdown to island exploration.

Transportation

Airfare: Your Gateway to Paradise

Most visitors touch down at Pointe-à-Pitre International Airport (PTP) on the island of Grande-Terre. Major airlines offer regular flights from North America, Europe, and the Caribbean. Prices fluctuate depending on the season, so booking in advance can snag you a better deal.

Island Hopping: Ferries for the Adventurous Soul

Guadeloupe isn't just one island, it's a delightful archipelago! Ferries connect the main islands of Basse-Terre and Grande-Terre, as well as other gems like Les Saintes and Marie-Galante. Schedules and fares vary by company and route, so research your options beforehand. The main ferry terminal is located in Pointe-à-Pitre, with additional terminals on other islands.

Hitting the Road: Car Rentals for Independent Explorers

Craving the freedom to explore at your own pace? Renting a car is a popular option. International driver's licenses are recommended, and most major car rental companies have offices at the airport and around the islands. Rates depend on the size and type of vehicle, so shop around for the best deal. Remember, Guadeloupe drives on the right side of the road.

Taxis: A Convenient (But Costlier) Option

Taxis are easily accessible at the airport and tourist locations. While convenient, they can be more expensive than alternative solutions. To avoid surprises, agree on a fare in advance. Taxis typically use meters, but it's always good to confirm the rate before getting in. Tipping is not mandatory, but a small gratuity is always appreciated for good service.

Buses: The Budget-Friendly Way to Go

Guadeloupe's bus system, called Karu'LIS, offers a budget-friendly way to get around, particularly on the main islands of Grande-Terre and Basse-Terre. Buses are colorful and generally reliable, but schedules can be less frequent outside of major towns. Fares are very reasonable, and you can pay the driver with exact change or small bills. Look for blue bus stops with route information displayed.

Island Shuttles: Shared Rides for a Social Experience

Several private companies offer shared shuttle services between the airport, hotels, and popular tourist destinations. This can be a cost-effective option, especially for small groups, and allows you to meet fellow travelers. Book your shuttle service ahead of time, especially during the busiest season.

Exploring on Foot and by Bike: The Eco-Friendly Approach

Many coastal towns and Pointe-à-Pitre are pedestrian-friendly, allowing you to explore at your own pace and soak up the local atmosphere. If you're staying near a beach, renting a bike is a fantastic way to explore the coastline and hidden coves. Several hotels and rental shops offer bicycle rentals.

Remember: Guadeloupe is a relatively small island chain, so getting around is manageable. Choose the transportation option that best suits your budget and travel style, and get ready to discover the magic of Guadeloupe!

CHAPTER 2. Regions of Guadeloupe

Grande-Terre

Grande-Terre, the larger of Guadeloupe's two main islands, is a playground for sun worshippers, water enthusiasts, and culture seekers. Picture this: powdery white beaches lapped by turquoise waters, swaying palm trees lining the coast, and charming towns brimming with French-Creole flair. Here's a glimpse into what awaits you in Grande-Terre:

Sun-Kissed Shores and Beach Bliss

Grande-Terre boasts some of Guadeloupe's most picture-perfect beaches. Let's dive into a few gems:

La Grande Anse: This expansive beach near Deshaies is a haven for water sports enthusiasts. Go kayaking, windsurfing, or simply relax on the golden sand.

Salines Beach: Fringed by swaying coconut palms and calm waters, Salines is ideal for families and those seeking a serene escape. Beach bars and restaurants line the shore for post-swim refreshments.

Sainte-Anne Bay: This horseshoe-shaped bay offers a string of delightful beaches, including Plage de la Caravelle and Plage de Bois Jolan. Enjoy swimming, snorkeling, or simply soaking up the Caribbean sunshine.

Beyond the Beach: Unveiling Grande-Terre's Treasures

While the beaches are undeniably captivating, Grande-Terre offers more than just sun and sand. Here are some hidden gems to discover:

- Pointe des Châteaux: This dramatic cliffside offers breathtaking panoramic views of the island. Hike the scenic trails, explore hidden coves, and soak up the dramatic scenery. There's a small entry fee to access the Pointe des Châteaux site.
- Pointe-à-Pitre:Guadeloupe's capital city is a vibrant hub with a rich history. Explore the bustling markets, visit the Schoelcher Museum (Musée Schoelcher) showcasing Caribbean art and artifacts (closed Mondays), or stroll along the scenic waterfront. Entrance to the Schoelcher Museum is free. It's open Tuesday through Saturday from 9:00 AM to 5:0 PM and Sundays from 9:00 AM to 1:00 PM.

- Distillerie Damoiseau: Immerse yourself in the world of rum production at this renowned distillery. Take a guided tour (offered for a fee) and learn about the rum-making process, followed by a delicious tasting.

Foodie Delights: A Taste of Grande-Terre

No Guadeloupe adventure is complete without indulging in its culinary scene. Grande-Terre offers a delightful mix of French and Creole flavors. Sample fresh seafood dishes, savor flavorful stews, and don't miss the chance to try a warm pain au chocolat (chocolate croissant) for breakfast.

Where to Stay:

Grande-Terre boasts a wide range of accommodation options, from luxurious beachfront resorts to charming guesthouses. Choose what suits your budget and travel style - whether it's a lively hotel on the marina or a secluded beachfront bungalow.

Grande-Terre awaits with its sun-drenched shores, cultural gems, and irresistible charm. So pack your swimsuit, grab your sense of adventure, and get ready to discover this captivating island paradise!

Basse-Terre

Basse-Terre, Guadeloupe's western island, is a nature lover's paradise. Imagine this: a majestic volcano cloaked in emerald rainforest, cascading waterfalls hidden within lush valleys, and black sand beaches whispering secrets of the sea. Basse-Terre is where Guadeloupe's wild soul thrives.

Volcanic Majesty: Hiking La Soufrière

Looming large over Basse-Terre is La Soufrière, a still-active volcano that last erupted in 1976. For adventurous souls, conquering the 1,467-meter (4,813-foot) peak is an unforgettable experience. Guided hikes are available for a fee, offering breathtaking panoramic views and a glimpse into the island's volcanic heart.

Waterfall Wonders: Chasing Cascades

Basse-Terre boasts a network of cascading waterfalls, each with its unique charm. Here are a couple not to miss:

- Carbet Falls (Chutes du Carbet): This series of three cascading falls within Guadeloupe National Park is a must-see. Take a refreshing dip in the pool at the base of the falls or simply marvel at the cascading water surrounded by lush greenery. There's a small park entrance fee to access the falls.

- Écrevisses Falls (Cascade aux Écrevisses): Tucked away near the town of Bouillante, this hidden gem offers a refreshing escape. Hike through the rainforest to reach the base of the falls and cool off with a swim in the crystal-clear pool.

Underwater Adventures: Marine Marvels Await

Basse-Terre's underwater world is a kaleidoscope of color. Head to Cousteau Reserve near Malendure for exceptional snorkeling and diving opportunities. Explore vibrant coral reefs teeming with tropical fish, playful sea turtles, and other marine wonders.

Thermal Delights: Soaking in Nature's Hot Springs

Basse-Terre is dotted with natural hot springs, offering a chance to relax and rejuvenate in steaming volcanic pools. The hot springs near Bouillante are particularly popular, where visitors can bathe in mineral-rich waters surrounded by lush vegetation.

Beyond Nature: Unveiling Basse-Terre's Treasures

While nature takes center stage, Basse-Terre offers cultural pockets to explore. Here are some interesting places to explore

- Deshaies Botanical Garden: Immerse yourself in a world of exotic flora at this botanical garden. Wander through themed gardens boasting orchids, bromeliads, and towering palm trees. There's a small entrance fee to access the garden. It's open from 9:00 AM to 5:00 PM.
- Fort Delgrès: Step back in time at this 18th-century fort overlooking the harbor of Basse-Terre. Explore the ramparts, learn about the island's history, and enjoy panoramic island views. Entry to the fort is free, and it's open daily from 9:00 AM to 5:00 PM.

Foodie Delights: A Taste of Basse-Terre

Basse-Terre's cuisine reflects its natural bounty. Sample fresh seafood dishes like grilled langoustine (spiny lobster) or flavorful Creole stews. Don't miss the chance to try local fruits like guava, mango, and passion fruit, bursting with tropical flavor.

Where to Stay:

Basse-Terre offers a variety of accommodation options, from charming eco-lodges nestled in the rainforest to boutique hotels with stunning ocean views. Choose what suits your budget and travel style, whether it's a rustic cabin near a waterfall or a beachfront bungalow with direct access to the ocean.

Basse-Terre beckons with its dramatic landscapes, hidden waterfalls, and volcanic allure. So lace up your hiking boots, grab your snorkel, and get ready to explore the wild heart of Guadeloupe!

Les Saintes

Les Saintes, a sprinkle of eight idyllic islands south of Guadeloupe, offers a laid-back island escape steeped in French charm. Imagine colorful Creole houses clinging to hillsides, turquoise bays lapped by gentle waves, and a pace of life that's delightfully slow. Here's a glimpse into what awaits you in this island paradise:

Island Hopping Adventure: Exploring Les Saintes Gems

Most visitors set foot on Terre-de-Haut, the largest inhabited island in Les Saintes. But for the adventurous soul, island hopping is a must. Day trips can be arranged to explore neighboring islands like Terre-de-Bas, known for its wild beauty and secluded beaches, or Ilet à Cabrit, a tiny island with a historic fort offering panoramic views.

Unwinding on Picture-Perfect Beaches

Les Saintes boasts some of Guadeloupe's most captivating beaches. Here are a couple of favorites:

- Pompierre Beach: This sheltered cove near Terre-de-Haut's main town is ideal for families. Relax on the soft sand, swim in the calm waters, or rent kayaks for a gentle paddle.
- Sugar Loaf Beach (Anse du Pain de Sucre): Accessible by a short hike, this secluded beach rewards visitors with pristine white sand and crystal-clear waters. Perfect for a tranquil escape.
- A Journey Through History: Fort Napoleon Perched atop a hill overlooking Terre-de-Haut, Fort Napoleon offers a glimpse into the island's rich history. Explore the ramparts, learn about the fort's role in defending the island, and enjoy breathtaking panoramic views. There's a small entrance fee to access the fort. Opening time: 9:00 AM to 5:00 PM.

Charming Strolls: Unveiling Terre-de-Hauts Heart

The main town of Terre-de-Haut is a delight to explore on foot. Wander through narrow streets lined with colorful Creole houses, browse charming boutiques for souvenirs, and savor a leisurely lunch at a waterfront cafe, watching the world go by.

A Culinary Adventure: Savoring Local Delights

Les Saintes' culinary scene is a delectable blend of French and Creole influences. Indulge in fresh seafood dishes like grilled lobster or flavorful Colombo curries. Don't miss the chance to try the local specialty, "Tourment d'Amour" (Lover's Torment), a flaky pastry filled with guava or coconut.

Where to Stay:

Les Saintes offers a variety of intimate accommodation options, from charming guesthouses nestled in the hills to boutique hotels with stunning ocean views. Choose what suits your budget and travel style, whether it's a cozy room in a traditional Creole house or a beachfront bungalow with direct access to the water.

Les Saintes beckons with its island charm, pristine beaches, and laid-back atmosphere. So ditch your watch, embrace the slow pace, and get ready to discover this captivating archipelago escape!

Marie-Galante

Marie-Galante, the "Big Galette" south of Guadeloupe, offers a taste of Guadeloupe's rural soul. Picture rolling hills covered in sugar cane fields, charming villages with colorful bungalows, and a laid-back pace of life that invites you to slow down and savor the moment. Here's a sneak peek of what awaits you on this Beautiful island:

A Journey Through Time: Windmills of Yesterday

Dotting the landscape of Marie-Galante are the remnants of a bygone era – towering windmills, once used to crush sugar cane. Explore these historical landmarks, some restored and even operational, offering a glimpse into the island's rich agricultural heritage. Most windmills are free to explore, though a few might have a small entrance fee.

Beach Bliss: Unveiling Marie Galante's Coastline

Marie-Galante boasts a string of beautiful beaches, each with its unique character. Here are a couple not to miss:

- Grande Anse des Galets: This expansive beach near Capesterre is a haven for water sports enthusiasts. Go windsurfing, kitesurfing, or simply relax on the black sand beach and soak up the dramatic scenery.

- Saline Beach: This horseshoe-shaped cove near Grand Bourg offers calm, turquoise waters ideal for swimming and snorkeling. Beachside restaurants and bars provide refreshments after a refreshing dip.

Beyond the Beach: Unveiling Marie Galante's Treasures

While beaches are a major draw, Marie-Galante offers more to explore. Here are a couple of fascinating stops:

- Distillery Bielle: Immerse yourself in the world of rum production at this renowned distillery. Take a guided tour (offered for a fee) and learn about the rum-making process, followed by a delicious tasting.
- Gueule Grand Gouffre: This natural wonder, meaning "Big Throat of the Abyss," is a dramatic chasm carved by the sea. Hike to the viewpoint and marvel at the power of nature as waves crash against the rugged cliffs. There's a small parking lot near the viewpoint, and the site itself is free to access.

Foodie Delights: A Taste of Marie-Galante

Marie-Galante's cuisine reflects its agricultural bounty. Sample fresh seafood dishes like grilled conch or flavorful stews incorporating local vegetables and spices. Don't miss the chance to try the island's famous "blanc manger," a coconut-based dessert with a light and creamy texture.

Local Rhythms: Experiencing the Culture

Marie-Galante takes pride in its cultural heritage. If you're lucky enough to be visiting during the annual "Terre de Blues" festival in May, you'll be treated to a vibrant celebration of blues music. Throughout the year, local artisans showcase their crafts at colorful markets, offering a chance to take home a unique piece of the island.

Where to Stay:

Marie-Galante offers a variety of intimate accommodation options. Choose from charming guesthouses nestled in villages to rustic beachfront bungalows for a truly laid-back experience. Some small hotels offer traditional Creole meals, allowing you to fully immerse yourself in the island's culture.

Marie-Galante beckons with its rolling hills, historical windmills, and laid-back charm. So escape the crowds, embrace the island's slow pace, and discover a captivating slice of Guadeloupe's rural soul!

La Désirade

La Désirade, aptly named "The Desired One," rises from the Guadeloupe archipelago like a rugged gem. Imagine a dramatic silhouette against the turquoise canvas, a landscape sculpted by wind and waves, and a pace of life that's refreshingly unhurried. Here's a taste of what awaits on this wild and captivating island:

Untamed Beauty: Hiking Dramatic Cliffs

La Désirade's crown jewel is its untamed nature. Lace up your hiking boots and explore the island's many trails, offering breathtaking panoramic views and a chance to commune with nature. The most challenging hike, La Grande Trace, traverses the island's ridgeline, rewarding you with unforgettable vistas. Remember, sturdy shoes and plenty of water are essential.

Sun-Kissed Shores: Unveiling Secluded Beaches

While not as extensive as other Guadeloupe islands, La Désirade boasts a handful of beautiful beaches, each with its charm. Here are a couple of favorites:

Souffleur Beach: This sheltered cove near the main town is ideal for families. Relax on the golden sand, swim in the calm waters, or simply soak up the sunshine.

- Fifi Beach: Accessible by a short walk, this secluded beach is a haven for tranquility. Picture white sand, turquoise waters, and a backdrop of dramatic cliffs – perfect for a peaceful escape.

A Step Back in Time: Exploring La Désirade's Past

La Désirade's history unfolds in its charming villages and historical sites. Wander through the main town, Désirade, with its colorful Creole houses and friendly locals. Explore the ruins of the Cotton Factory, a reminder of the island's bygone industrial past. Most historical sites are free to explore, though some might have a small donation box for upkeep.

Whispers of the Sea: Visiting the Whale Sanctuary

La Désirade sits within the Agoa Marine Mammal Sanctuary, making it a prime spot for whale watching (between December and April). Embark on a boat trip (tours can be arranged locally for a fee) and keep your eyes peeled for majestic humpback whales migrating through crystal-clear waters.

A Culinary Adventure: Savoring Local Delights

La Désirade's cuisine is all about fresh, local ingredients. Sample freshly caught fish grilled to perfection, flavorful stews incorporating island vegetables, and don't miss the chance to try the local "langouste flambée" (flambéed spiny lobster) – a fiery culinary delight.

Where to Stay:

La Désirade offers a limited selection of accommodations, but that's part of its charm. Choose from small, family-run guesthouses nestled in the village to beachfront bungalows offering a true escape. Remember, this island caters to a more low-key experience, so don't expect sprawling resorts.

La Désirade beckons with its wild beauty, dramatic cliffs, and laid-back charm. So escape the crowds, embrace the island's untamed spirit, and discover a captivating piece of Guadeloupe waiting to be explored!

CHAPTER 3. Top Attractions in Guadeloupe

Guadeloupe's crown jewels are undoubtedly its beaches, boasting something for every beach bum. From calm coves ideal for families to dramatic stretches perfect for water sports enthusiasts, here are two captivating coastal escapes not to be missed:

Beaches and Coastal Areas

1. La Grande Anse (Deshaies): Paradise for Water Sports Enthusiasts

Nestled on the southwestern coast of Basse-Terre, La Grande Anse in Deshaies is a haven for active beach lovers. Imagine a long stretch of golden sand lapped by turquoise waters, framed by swaying palm trees. This beach is a playground for windsurfing, kayaking, and stand-up paddleboarding. Several vendors offer equipment rentals and lessons (for a fee) for those wanting to try their hand at these activities.

- Calm Waters and Family Fun: While the waves can pick up at times, the sheltered bay generally offers calm waters ideal for swimming and snorkeling. Relax on the soft sand, soak up the sunshine, or build sandcastles with the little ones.

- Beachside Bliss: A string of restaurants and bars line the beachfront, offering refreshing drinks and delicious local cuisine after a day of fun in the sun. Most restaurants have outdoor seating with stunning ocean views, making your meal a truly unforgettable experience. There's no entrance fee to access La Grande Anse beach, and it's open to the public year-round.

2. Salines Beach (Grande-Terre): Tranquility and Island Charm

Salines Beach on the southern tip of Grande-Terre is a vision of serenity. Picture a horseshoe-shaped cove with pristine white sand, calm turquoise waters whispering secrets, and a laid-back atmosphere perfect for unwinding. This beach is ideal for families with young children due to the gentle waves and shallow waters.

- Relaxation and Sunbathing: Stretch out on a beach lounger (rentals available for a fee) and soak up the Caribbean sunshine. The calm waters are perfect for a refreshing swim, or simply wade in and let the gentle waves lap at your feet.
- Upscale Touches: Several chic beach bars and restaurants dot the shoreline, offering a variety of refreshments and delicious food options. Some

even offer waiter service directly to your beach lounger, allowing you to relax in ultimate comfort. Salines Beach has no entrance fee and is open to the public year-round.

- Beyond the Beach: Both La Grande Anse and Salines Beach offer opportunities for exploration beyond the sand. La Grande Anse is a great starting point for hikes along the scenic Deshaies coastline, while Salines Beach is close to the Pointe des Chateaux with its dramatic cliffs and breathtaking views.

These are just two of Guadeloupe's many captivating coastal escapes. So grab your swimsuit, sunscreen, and sense of adventure, and get ready to discover your slice of paradise on the shores of this enchanting island!

National Parks and Nature Reserves

Guadeloupe's true wild soul resides in its national parks and nature reserves. Lush rainforests teeming with life, volcanic peaks scraping the sky, and cascading waterfalls hidden within emerald valleys – these protected areas offer a chance to immerse yourself in the island's breathtaking natural beauty. Here are two not-to-miss treasures:

1. Guadeloupe National Park (Basse-Terre): A Paradise for Hikers and Nature Lovers

Encompassing a vast swathe of Basse-Terre's landscape, Guadeloupe National Park is a hiker's paradise. Picture a network of well-maintained trails winding through a rainforest, leading you past hidden waterfalls, volcanic peaks, and a diverse array of flora and fauna.

- Volcanic Majesty: The park's crown jewel is La Soufrière, a still-active volcano that last erupted in 1976. Conquering this 1,467-meter (4,813-foot) peak is a challenging yet rewarding experience for seasoned hikers. Guided tours are available for a fee and offer a safe and informative way to explore the volcano's slopes.
- Waterfall Wonders: The park boasts several cascading waterfalls, each with its unique charm. The easily accessible Carbet Falls (Chutes du Carbet) are a must-see. Hike through lush vegetation and take a refreshing dip in the cool pool beneath the cascading waters. There's a small park entrance fee to access the falls.
- Exploring the Coast: The park also encompasses a portion of Basse-Terre's rugged coastline. Hike along scenic trails offering dramatic ocean views, or explore hidden coves accessible only by foot.
- Park Information: The park headquarters are located in Basse-Terre city. There's a small

entrance fee to access most areas of the park. The park is open year-round, though some trails might be closed due to weather conditions. It's best to check with park authorities before setting off on your adventure.

2. Grand Cul-de-Sac Marin Nature Reserve (Grande-Terre): A Haven for Marine Life

Located on the southeastern tip of Grande-Terre, Grand Cul-de-Sac Marin Nature Reserve is a haven for water enthusiasts and nature lovers. Picture a vast mangrove lagoon teeming with marine life, crystal-clear waters perfect for snorkeling, and a tranquil atmosphere ideal for escaping the crowds.

- Underwater Paradise: The calm waters of the lagoon are a snorkeler's dream. Explore vibrant coral reefs teeming with colorful fish, playful sea turtles, and other marine wonders. Several companies offer guided snorkeling tours (for a fee) for those wanting to explore the underwater world with a knowledgeable guide.
- Island Hopping Adventure: The nature reserve also encompasses several offshore islets, some accessible by boat tours. Explore hidden coves, and pristine beaches, and witness unique wildlife on these uninhabited islands.

- Kayaking Paradise: The calm waters of the lagoon are perfect for a leisurely kayaking adventure. Rent a kayak (available for a fee from local vendors) and explore hidden mangrove channels, spot colorful birds amongst the lush vegetation, and enjoy the serenity of the nature reserve.
- Nature Reserve Information: There's no entrance fee to access the Grand Cul-de-Sac Marin Nature Reserve. However, some water activities like guided tours and kayak rentals might incur a fee. The nature reserve is open year-round, but weather conditions can sometimes impact accessibility.

Guadeloupe's national parks and nature reserves offer something for every nature lover. So lace up your hiking boots, grab your snorkel, and get ready to discover the breathtaking beauty of this captivating island!

Historic Sites and Museums

Guadeloupe boasts a rich and complex history, reflected in its captivating historic sites and museums. From exploring remnants of a bygone colonial era to learning about the island's unique cultural heritage, these gems offer a glimpse into Guadeloupe's fascinating past. Here are two not-to-miss experiences for history buffs:

1. Mémorial ACTe (Pointe-à-Pitre): A Poignant Exploration of Slavery

The Mémorial ACTe, situated in Pointe-à-Pitre, Guadeloupe's capital city, is a powerful and moving tribute to the victims of slavery. Imagine a striking silver-latticework building housing an expansive museum dedicated to exploring the transatlantic slave trade and its lasting impact on Guadeloupe and the wider Caribbean region.

- A Journey Through History: Permanent and temporary exhibits delve into the horrors of the slave trade, the fight for freedom, and the enduring legacy of slavery on Guadeloupe's culture and society. Interactive displays, historical artifacts, and multimedia presentations bring the past to life, encouraging reflection and understanding.
- A Must-See for All: The Mémorial ACTe is a thought-provoking and essential stop for anyone wanting to gain a deeper understanding of Guadeloupe's history. It serves as a powerful reminder of the struggles of the past and a call for a brighter future.

Location and Information: The Mémorial ACTe is located at Pointe-à-Pitre's harbor forefront. There's an entrance fee to access the museum, and it's open Tuesday through Saturday from 9:00 AM to 5:00 PM and Sundays from 9:00AM

2.Domaine de Deshaies (Deshaies): A Step Back in Time to Colonial Elegance

Nestled amidst the lush gardens of Deshaies, on Basse-Terre, lies the Domaine de Deshaies, a captivating historical site offering a glimpse into Guadeloupe's colonial past. Imagine a beautifully restored 17th-century sugar plantation, complete with grand colonial houses, meticulously maintained gardens and remnants of the island's once-thriving sugar industry.

- Exploring the Plantation Grounds: Wander through the manicured gardens, adorned with colorful flowers and towering palm trees. Step inside the restored plantation houses, filled with period furniture and artifacts that offer a window into the lives of the plantation owners. Learn about the sugar production process and the role it played in shaping Guadeloupe's history.
- A Family-Friendly Adventure: The Domaine de Deshaies is a perfect destination for a family outing. Kids will be enthralled by the historic setting, while adults can appreciate the site's historical significance. Guided tours (offered for a fee) provide a deeper understanding of the plantation's past.

- Location and Information: The Domaine de Deshaies is located in Deshaies, Basse-Terre. There's an entrance fee to access the grounds, and it's open daily from 9:00 AM to 5:00 PM.

These are just two of Guadeloupe's many captivating historic sites and museums. So delve into the island's fascinating past, explore these captivating gems, and gain a deeper appreciation for the rich tapestry woven into the heart of Guadeloupe!

Culinary Experiences

Guadeloupe's charm extends far beyond its stunning landscapes. Immerse yourself in the island's vibrant culture through its captivating cuisine, a unique blend of French, African, and Indian influences. Here are two culinary experiences not to be missed:

1. Exploring Local Markets: A Feast for the Senses

Guadeloupe's bustling markets are a haven for foodies. Imagine vibrant stalls overflowing with fresh, local produce – colorful fruits and vegetables, plump seafood glistening in the sunshine, and an intoxicating aroma of spices wafting through the air. These markets are a feast for the senses and a gateway to authentic Guadeloupean flavors.

- A Treasure Trove of Ingredients: Stroll through the market and discover an array of exotic ingredients. Sample juicy mangoes, tangy guavas, and starfruit, unlike anything you've tasted before. Select plump, freshly caught fish for your evening meal, or pick up fragrant spices like nutmeg, cloves, and cinnamon to infuse your dishes with a Caribbean flair.
- Local Specialties: Don't miss the chance to try some of Guadeloupe's signature dishes. Sample "Colombo," a flavorful curry dish traditionally made with chicken or seafood. Bite into a savory "BoKit," a deep-fried sandwich filled with meat, cheese, and vegetables. And for dessert, indulge in "Tourment d'Amour" (Lover's Torment), a flaky pastry filled with guava or coconut, guaranteed to tantalize your taste buds.
- Market Locations and Information: Most towns and villages in Guadeloupe have their market days, typically held in the mornings. Popular markets include the Marché aux épices (Spice Market) in Pointe-à-Pitre and the Marché de Basse-Terre, known for its fresh seafood selection. There's no entrance fee to explore the markets, and opening times can vary depending on the location.

2. Cooking Class with a Local Chef: Unveiling Culinary Secrets

For a truly immersive experience, sign up for a cooking class with a local chef. Imagine learning the secrets of Guadeloupean cuisine in a relaxed and friendly setting. Under the guidance of an experienced chef, you'll learn traditional cooking techniques, discover the history behind local dishes, and most importantly, have fun creating your culinary masterpieces.

- Hands-on Learning: These classes typically involve a trip to a local market to select fresh ingredients, followed by a hands-on cooking session where you'll learn to prepare several Guadeloupean dishes. The highlight is undoubtedly enjoying the fruits (or should we say vegetables?) of your labor – a delicious meal savored with your fellow classmates and the chef.
- Finding a Cooking Class: Several companies offer cooking classes in Guadeloupe, catering to all skill levels. Most can be booked online or directly through your hotel concierge. Prices can vary depending on the duration and complexity of the class.

Embrace the spirit of discovery and embark on a culinary adventure in Guadeloupe. From bustling markets to intimate cooking classes, prepare to tantalize your taste buds and create lasting memories through the island's captivating cuisine!

CHAPTER 4. Outdoor Activities

Guadeloupe's volcanic peaks, lush rainforests, and dramatic coastlines offer a paradise for hikers and trekkers of all levels. Imagine challenging climbs rewarding you with breathtaking panoramic views, tranquil rainforest trails teeming with life, and coastal paths unveiling hidden coves. Here are two hikes not to be missed:

Hiking and Trekking

1. Conquering La Soufrière (Basse-Terre): A Challenge for Experienced Hikers

For seasoned adventurers, scaling La Soufrière, Guadeloupe's highest peak, is the ultimate challenge. This still-active volcano (last erupted in 1976) offers a demanding yet unforgettable trek. Picture a steep and often rugged trail winding its way through verdant rainforest, leading you past steaming fumaroles and volcanic rock formations.

- Reaching the Summit: The hike typically takes a full day, requiring a good level of fitness and proper preparation. The reward for your efforts? Breathtaking panoramic views encompass the entire island, neighboring islands peeking out from the horizon, and the dramatic crater spewing wisps of steam.

- Important Information: Given the challenging nature of the hike, it's highly recommended to tackle La Soufrière with a certified guide. Guides can be booked through local tour operators for a fee. The park headquarters in Basse-Terre city can provide information on trail conditions and safety precautions. There's a small entrance fee to access Guadeloupe National Park, which encompasses La Soufrière. The park is generally open year-round, though weather conditions can sometimes impact accessibility.

2. Trace des Esclaves (Basse-Terre): A Journey Through History and Nature

For a more moderate yet historically significant hike, explore the Trace des Esclaves (Slave Trail). Imagine a well-maintained trail winding through a lush rainforest, following the path once used by enslaved people to access higher grounds. This hike offers a glimpse into the island's past while showcasing the beauty of the rainforest ecosystem.

- A Walk Through Time: Interpretive signs along the trail tell the story of slavery in Guadeloupe, adding a layer of poignancy to the hike. Keep an

eye out for diverse flora and fauna along the way
– colorful birds flitting through the trees, exotic
plant life, and maybe even a glimpse of a
scurrying mongoose.

- Exploring Further: The Trace des Esclaves can be
tackled as a shorter out-and-back hike or as part
of a longer trek through the national park.
Several waterfalls and scenic viewpoints are
accessible along the trail.
- Location and Information: The Trace des
Esclaves starts near Deux Mamelles, a prominent
landmark in Basse-Terre. There's no entrance fee
to access the trail, and it's open year-round.
However, some sections might be closed due to
weather conditions, so checking with park
authorities before setting off is recommended.

These are just two of the many captivating hikes and
treks Guadeloupe offers. So lace up your boots, grab
your backpack, and get ready to explore the island's
stunning landscapes on foot!

Watersports (Snorkeling, Scuba Diving, Surfing)

Guadeloupe's crystal-clear waters and vibrant marine life
make it a haven for watersports enthusiasts. Imagine
exploring underwater coral gardens teeming with

colorful fish, riding thrilling waves, or gliding serenely through turquoise bays. Here are two aquatic adventures not to be missed:

1. Unveiling the Underwater World: Snorkeling and Scuba Diving Paradise

Guadeloupe boasts a treasure trove of dive sites, catering to both novice snorkelers and experienced scuba divers. Picture vibrant coral reefs teeming with life – from playful parrotfish and graceful angelfish to majestic sea turtles and curious octopuses.

- A Snorkeler's Dream: Several calm bays and coves offer ideal snorkeling conditions. Grab a mask, fins, and snorkel (available for rent at most beaches for a fee) and explore the underwater world right from the shore. Colorful coral formations, shimmering schools of fish, and playful sea creatures await you just beneath the surface.
- Diving Deeper: For certified scuba divers, Guadeloupe offers a world of underwater exploration. Wreck dives, teeming with marine life, sheer walls plunging into the abyss, and vibrant coral reefs teeming with tropical fish are just a few of the underwater wonders. Several dive companies offer guided tours (for a fee) to

the best dive sites, ensuring a safe and unforgettable experience.

- Popular Dive Sites: Some of the most popular dive sites include Cousteau Reserve in Pigeon Island (Grande-Terre), Jacques Cousteau National Park (covering parts of both islands), and wrecks like the Bianca C: a Swedish ferry resting on the seabed near Pointe-à-Pitre.

2. Taming the Waves: A Surfer's Paradise

Guadeloupe's consistent trade winds and rolling waves make it a surfer's paradise. Imagine catching thrilling waves on pristine beaches, surrounded by lush landscapes and turquoise waters. Whether you're a seasoned surfer or a curious beginner, Guadeloupe offers something for everyone.

- Catching the Perfect Wave: Several beaches boast ideal surfing conditions. Popular spots include La Grande Anse in Deshaies (Basse-Terre) with its powerful waves, and Moule (Grande-Terre) with its consistent swells and protected coves ideal for beginners.
- Learning to Ride: Surf schools offer lessons (for a fee) for those wanting to learn the basics or improve their skills. Experienced instructors will guide you through the fundamentals of surfing,

ensuring a safe and enjoyable introduction to this exhilarating sport.

- Surf Season: The best waves in Guadeloupe typically arrive between November and April, coinciding with the trade winds. However, some spots offer surfable waves year-round.
- Important Information: Always check surf conditions and rip currents before entering the water. Lifeguards are not present on all beaches, so it's important to exercise caution and surf responsibly.

These are just two of the many captivating watersports adventures Guadeloupe offers. So grab your swimsuit, sunscreen, and sense of adventure, and get ready to make a splash in the turquoise waters of this captivating island!

Sailing and Boat Tours

Guadeloupe's magic extends beyond its stunning beaches. Imagine exploring the island's dramatic coastline from the water, sailing past hidden coves, secluded islands, and vibrant coral reefs. Here are two captivating sailing and boat tour options to consider:

1. Island Hopping Adventure: Exploring Guadeloupe's Hidden Gems

Embark on an island-hopping adventure and discover the hidden treasures scattered around Guadeloupe. Picture a comfortable catamaran or sailboat gliding across turquoise waters, stopping at secluded islands accessible only by boat. Explore pristine beaches, snorkel vibrant coral reefs teeming with life, and soak up the serenity of untouched landscapes.

- Island Delights: Popular island-hopping tours might take you to gems like Les Saintes, an archipelago known for its charming villages, picturesque bays, and historical sites. Another option is Marie-Galante, the "Island of a Hundred Windmills," where you can explore rolling hills, and charming towns, and taste the island's renowned rum.
- A Day on the Water: These tours typically last for a half-day or a full day, offering plenty of time for swimming, snorkeling, sunbathing, and exploring the islands you visit. Lunch is often included onboard the boat, featuring fresh, local cuisine.
- Booking Your Adventure: Several companies offer island-hopping tours, departing from various marinas in Guadeloupe, particularly Pointe-à-Pitre, Basse-Terre, and Grande-Terre. Prices can vary depending on the duration, itinerary, and the type of boat. It is suggested that

you book in advance, especially during the high season.

2. Sunset Sail: A Romantic End to the Day

For a truly unforgettable experience, set sail on a sunset cruise. Imagine gliding across the calm evening waters as the sun dips below the horizon, painting the sky in fiery hues of orange, pink, and purple. Enjoy refreshing drinks and delicious snacks onboard as you soak up the breathtaking scenery and the romantic ambiance.

- A Moment of Tranquility: Sunset cruises are perfect for couples seeking a romantic escape or for families wanting to unwind after a day of exploration. These cruises typically last for a few hours, offering a relaxing and scenic way to end the day.
- Finding a Sunset Sail: Most marinas in Guadeloupe offer sunset cruises, especially during peak season. Prices can vary depending on the duration, the type of boat, and any food or drinks included. It's best to book in advance, especially if you're traveling during peak season.

Sailing and boat tours offer a unique way to experience the magic of Guadeloupe. So set sail, feel the gentle breeze in your hair, and discover the island's hidden gems and captivating beauty from a whole new perspective!

Birdwatching and Wildlife Viewing

Guadeloupe isn't just about stunning beaches and volcanic peaks; it's a haven for birdwatchers and wildlife enthusiasts. Imagine lush rainforests echoing with the calls of exotic birds, vibrant plumage flitting through the trees, and unique creatures hiding amongst the greenery. Here are two captivating birding and wildlife-viewing experiences not to be missed:

1. Exploring Guadeloupe National Park: A Symphony of Birdlife

Encompassing a vast swathe of Basse-Terre, Guadeloupe National Park is a treasure trove for birdwatchers. Picture a network of well-maintained trails winding through a rainforest, leading you past hidden waterfalls and volcanic peaks – all while offering the chance to spot an incredible array of feathered friends.

- A Chorus of Colors: The park boasts over 260 bird species, a symphony of colors and calls filling the air. Keep an eye out for the vibrantly colored endemic Guadeloupe Woodpecker, the elusive Forest Thrush with its haunting song, and the graceful frigatebirds soaring effortlessly on thermal currents.

- Beyond the Birds: The park isn't just for bird lovers. Keep your eyes peeled for agile iguanas basking on sun-drenched rocks, curious agoutis (rodents) scurrying through the undergrowth, and the occasional glimpse of the elusive mongoose.
- Park Information: The park headquarters are located in Basse-Terre city. There's a small entrance fee to access most areas of the park. The park is open year-round, though some trails might be closed due to weather conditions. Consider hiring a local birding guide (available for a fee) to enhance your experience and learn more about the park's diverse birdlife.

2. Pointe des Châteaux (Grande-Terre): Dramatic Cliffs and Soaring Seabirds

For a different kind of wildlife experience, head to the dramatic cliffs of Pointe des Châteaux on Grande-Terre. Imagine rugged cliffs sculpted by wind and waves, offering breathtaking ocean views and a chance to spot magnificent seabirds soaring on the currents.

- A Feast for the Eyes: Keep your binoculars handy and scan the skies for frigatebirds with their impressive wingspans, graceful boobies diving for fish, and playful terns flitting amongst the waves. On the cliffs themselves, you might spot tropicbirds with their distinctive long tail feathers and red-footed boobies nesting in the crevices.

- Exploring Further: Pointe des Châteaux offers scenic hiking trails, perfect for exploring the dramatic landscape and enjoying panoramic views. Keep an eye out for interesting tide pools teeming with marine life at the base of the cliffs.

- Location and Information: Pointe des Châteaux is located on the eastern tip of Grande-Terre. There's no entrance fee to access the site, and it's open year-round. Be aware of strong winds and slippery rocks along the cliffs.

Guadeloupe offers a unique opportunity to experience a vibrant tapestry of birdlife and fascinating wildlife. So grab your binoculars, a healthy dose of patience, and get ready to be amazed by the island's natural wonders!

CHAPTER 5. Cultural Experiences

Guadeloupe's cultural spirit comes alive during its captivating festivals and events. Imagine pulsating music filling the air, streets teeming with colorfully dressed locals, and the intoxicating aroma of delicious food wafting through the crowds. Here are two vibrant celebrations not to be missed:

Local Festivals and Events

1. Carnival: A Celebration of Life, Music, and Colors (January-February)

Guadeloupe's Carnival, held annually from January to February, is a vibrant explosion of life, music, and color. Picture costumed revelers parading through the streets in elaborate costumes, rhythmic drumbeats echoing in the air, and a contagious energy that sweeps everyone into the celebratory spirit.

- A Feast for the Senses: The weeks leading up to Carnival are filled with lively pre-Carnival events, known as "déboulé" (literally "unleashed"). Join the throngs of locals dancing in the streets, witness colorful parades showcasing elaborate costumes, and be mesmerized by the infectious energy. Carnival culminates in a series of parades, culminating in "Mardi Gras" (Fat Tuesday), a day of unbridled revelry before the somber mood of Ash Wednesday sets in.

- Where to Experience Carnival: Carnival celebrations take place across Guadeloupe, with the biggest festivities happening in Pointe-à-Pitre, Basse-Terre, and Moule. While there's no entrance fee to witness the festivities, some events like costume balls might require tickets.

2. Fête des Saints (All Saints' Day): Honoring Ancestral Traditions (November 1st)

Fête des Saints, held on November 1st, is a poignant and beautiful celebration honoring ancestors. Picture families gathering at cemeteries, decorating graves with colorful flowers and candles, and sharing stories and memories of loved ones who have passed away.

- A Time for Reflection: This deeply rooted tradition offers a glimpse into Guadeloupean culture and its reverence for ancestors. While somber, it's also a time for families to come together, share meals, and celebrate the lives of those who came before them.

- Experiencing the Celebration: Fête des Saints is observed throughout Guadeloupe, with cemeteries being the central focus of the festivities. It's a respectful observation rather than a tourist spectacle, so be mindful of local customs and traditions.

These are just two of the many captivating festivals and events that Guadeloupe offers. So immerse yourself in the island's vibrant culture, pulsating music, and rich traditions, and create lasting memories during your Guadeloupean adventure!

Traditional Music and Dance

Guadeloupe's soul pulsates with the rhythm of its captivating traditional music and dance. Imagine infectious drumbeats echoing through the air, graceful dancers swaying to the music, and a vibrant energy that draws you into the heart of the island's culture. Here are two captivating ways to experience this rich heritage:

1. Gwoka Nights: Immerse Yourself in the Rhythm of Guadeloupe (Throughout the Year)

Gwoka, a pulsating blend of African and European influences, is the lifeblood of Guadeloupean music. Picture lively evening gatherings, known as "Gwoka nights," where skilled percussionists (tambouyés) beat out hypnotic rhythms on traditional "ka" drums. These gatherings are more than just performances; they're vibrant community events where everyone is welcome to participate.

- A Call to Dance: The infectious rhythms of Gwoka nights are a call to dance. Watch seasoned dancers showcase their graceful movements, or simply move to the beat and feel the energy of the music. Some evenings might even feature guest performers singing traditional songs in Guadeloupean Creole, adding another layer to the cultural immersion.
- Finding a Gwoka Night: Gwoka nights are held throughout the year in various locations across Guadeloupe, from restaurants and bars to community centers. Local tourist offices or your hotel concierge can provide information on upcoming events. There's typically a small entrance fee to cover the cost of the musicians.

2. Traditional Dance Performances: A Journey Through Guadeloupe's History (Varies)

For a more staged experience, attend a traditional dance performance. Imagine dancers adorned in colorful costumes, showcasing a variety of dance styles that tell stories of the island's rich history and cultural influences.

Witness the intricate steps of the Belemba, a dance with African roots, or be mesmerized by the elegant movements of the La Quadrille, a dance with European influences.

- A Cultural Mosaic: These performances offer a captivating window into Guadeloupe's diverse heritage. Learn about the stories behind the dances, the symbolism of the costumes, and the importance of tradition in Guadeloupean culture. Many performances are held at cultural centers or open-air venues.
- Finding a Performance: Traditional dance performances are not as frequent as Gwoka nights, but they are still held throughout the year, particularly during festivals and cultural events. Check with local tourist offices or cultural centers for upcoming performances. Ticket prices can vary depending on the venue and the production.

Guadeloupe's traditional music and dance offer a captivating portal into the island's soul. So tap your feet, sway to the rhythm, and immerse yourself in the vibrant cultural tapestry that awaits!

Arts and Crafts

Guadeloupe's artistic spirit extends beyond its captivating landscapes. Immerse yourself in the island's vibrant culture by exploring its unique arts and crafts scene. Imagine colorful paintings depicting island life, intricate sculptures whispering stories of the past, and handcrafted objects showcasing generations-old techniques. Here are two captivating ways to delve into this artistic haven:

1. Exploring Local Markets: A Treasure Trove of Creativity (Throughout the Year)

Guadeloupe's bustling markets are a treasure trove of local crafts. Picture overflowing stalls displaying an array of artistic creations – vibrant paintings capturing the island's beauty, intricately woven baskets brimming with fresh produce, and handcrafted jewelry adorned with colorful beads and seashells.

- A Feast for the Senses: Wander through the market and discover the work of local artisans. Admire the vibrant paintings depicting scenes of Guadeloupean life, the detailed wood carvings depicting island flora and fauna, and the delicate madras (cotton cloth) creations, a testament to the island's Indian heritage. Haggling is a common practice, so don't be afraid to put your bargaining skills to the test!

- Market Hopping: Most towns and villages in Guadeloupe have their market days, typically held in the mornings. Popular markets include the Marché aux épices (Spice Market) in Pointe-à-Pitre and the Marché de Basse-Terre, known for its selection of handcrafted souvenirs. There's no entrance fee to explore the markets, and opening times can vary depending on the location.

2. Visiting Local Artisan Studios: Unveiling the Creative Process (Varies)

For a deeper dive into the artistic soul of Guadeloupe, visit local artisan studios. Imagine stepping into a potter's workshop, watching skilled hands transform lumps of clay into beautiful ceramics. Witness a weaver patiently crafting intricate baskets using traditional techniques, or observe a sculptor meticulously carving a piece of wood into a captivating artwork.

- Meeting the Makers: Visiting studios allow you to meet the talented artisans behind the beautiful creations. Learn about their techniques, the stories behind their work, and the cultural significance of their art form. Many artisans are happy to answer your questions and share their passion for their craft.

- Finding a Studio: Local tourist offices or your hotel concierge can provide information on artisan studios open to the public. Some studios might require appointments for visits, while others welcome walk-ins. There's usually no entrance fee to visit studios, but some artisans might offer workshops or demonstrations for a fee.

Guadeloupe's arts and crafts scene offers a captivating glimpse into the island's creativity and cultural heritage. So embrace your inner art enthusiast, explore the vibrant markets and studios, and take home a unique piece of Guadeloupe to cherish for years to come!

CHAPTER 6. Food and Dining

Guadeloupe's charm extends far beyond its stunning landscapes. Immerse yourself in the island's vibrant culture through its captivating cuisine, a unique blend of French, African, and Indian influences. Imagine robust stews simmered with fragrant spices, fresh seafood dishes bursting with ocean flavors, and sweet treats that tantalize your taste buds. Here are two culinary experiences not to be missed:

Local Cuisine and Specialties

1. Exploring Local Restaurants: A Journey Through Flavor (Throughout the Year)

Guadeloupe's restaurants offer a chance to delve into the island's diverse culinary scene. Picture charming open-air eateries overlooking the turquoise waters, bustling family-run restaurants tucked away in hidden corners, and upscale establishments showcasing the talents of local chefs.

- A Gastronomic Adventure: No Guadeloupean culinary journey is complete without sampling some of the island's signature dishes. Savor a hearty bowl of "Colombo," a flavorful curry typically made with chicken or seafood. Bite into a savory "BoKit," a deep-fried sandwich filled with meat, cheese, and vegetables. And for dessert, indulge in "Tourment d'Amour" (Lover's Torment), a flaky pastry filled with guava or coconut, guaranteed to tantalize your taste buds.

- Finding the Perfect Bite: Guadeloupe offers a wide range of restaurants to suit all budgets and tastes. From casual beachfront shacks serving fresh seafood to upscale establishments with tasting menus, there's something for everyone. Local tourist offices or your hotel concierge can recommend restaurants catering to your preferences. Prices can vary depending on the restaurant's location and level of formality.

2. Taking a Cooking Class: Unveiling Culinary Secrets (Varies)

For a truly immersive experience, sign up for a cooking class with a local chef. Imagine learning the secrets of Guadeloupean cuisine in a relaxed and friendly setting. Under the guidance of an experienced chef, you'll learn traditional cooking techniques, discover the history behind local dishes, and most importantly, have fun creating your culinary masterpieces.

- Hands-on Learning: These classes typically involve a trip to a local market to select fresh ingredients, followed by a hands-on cooking session where you'll learn to prepare several Guadeloupean dishes. The highlight is undoubtedly enjoying the fruits (or should we say vegetables?) of your labor – a delicious meal savored with your fellow classmates and the chef.

- Booking a Class: Several companies offer cooking classes in Guadeloupe, catering to all skill levels. Most can be booked online or directly through your hotel concierge. Prices can vary depending on the duration and complexity of the class, but it's an investment that will leave you with lasting memories and newfound culinary skills.

Embrace the spirit of discovery and embark on a culinary adventure in Guadeloupe. From bustling restaurants to intimate cooking classes, prepare to tantalize your taste buds and create lasting memories through the island's captivating cuisine!

Popular Restaurants and Eateries

Guadeloupe's culinary scene is a delectable blend of French, African, and Indian influences, offering a delightful adventure for your taste buds. While the island boasts a wide range of restaurants to suit all budgets and preferences, here are a few standouts not to be missed:

Fine Dining with a View:

La Kaz à Pain (Deshaies): Nestled on the cliffs overlooking Deshaies Bay, La Kaz à Pain offers breathtaking ocean views and an upscale dining experience. Their menu showcases fresh, seasonal ingredients in innovative dishes, with a focus on local seafood. Expect a romantic ambiance and attentive service. (Pricey, Reservations recommended)

Hidden Gems for Local Flavor:

Chez Mamie Léone (Sainte-Anne): This charming, family-run restaurant in Sainte-Anne offers a delightful taste of authentic Creole cuisine. Tucked away in a side street, it serves generous portions of classic dishes like Colombo (stew) and Fricassée (chicken fricassee) at affordable prices. Be prepared for a taste of local life and friendly service. (Cash only)

Beachside Bliss:

Le Langoustier (Bouillante): This lively beachfront restaurant in Bouillante specializes in fresh seafood dishes – think grilled lobster, flavorful conch fritters, and daily catches prepared to perfection. Enjoy the laid-back atmosphere, the sound of waves lapping at the shore, and the stunning views of Pigeon Island. (Moderate prices)

Creperie Delights:

La Crêperie Bretonne (Pointe-à-Pitre): For a taste of France on a Caribbean island, head to La Crêperie Bretonne in Pointe-à-Pitre. This cozy eatery serves a wide variety of savory and sweet crêpes, made with fresh, local ingredients. It's a perfect spot for a casual lunch or a sweet afternoon treat. (Budget-friendly)

Street Food Feasts:

Marché aux épices (Spice Market) - Pointe-à-Pitre: Immerse yourself in the sights and smells of Guadeloupean street food at the bustling Marché aux épices in Pointe-à-Pitre. Sample savory samosas, succulent grilled chicken kebabs, and fresh tropical fruit from various vendors, all at affordable prices. Don't be afraid to bargain and soak up the vibrant market atmosphere. (Cash only)

Remember: This is just a small sampling of the delectable options Guadeloupe offers. Opening times and prices can vary, so it's always best to check with the restaurant directly before your visit. Many restaurants close on Sundays, so plan accordingly.

Embrace your inner foodie and embark on a culinary adventure in Guadeloupe!

CHAPTER 7. Practical Information

Planning a vacation to Guadeloupe? Understanding the island's currency and banking system will ensure a smooth and hassle-free experience. Here's an overview of everything you should know:

Currency and Banking

Guadeloupe's Currency:

The Euro (EUR): As a French territory, Guadeloupe uses the Euro as its official currency. This means you can use the Euros you have on hand or exchange your home currency for Euros before your trip.

Exchanging Money:

Airport Exchange Bureaus: Several currency exchange booths are located at Pointe-à-Pitre International Airport (PTP). Their rates might not be the most competitive, but they offer convenience upon arrival.

- Banks: Banks throughout Guadeloupe offer currency exchange services. Opening hours typically run from Monday to Friday, 8:00 AM to 4:00 PM, with some branches closed for lunch break. Banks generally offer better exchange rates than airport kiosks.

- ATMs: Widely available throughout the island, ATMs are a convenient way to withdraw Euros using your debit or credit card. Be sure to inform your bank about your travel plans to avoid blocked cards. Fees associated with international ATM withdrawals may apply, so check with your bank beforehand.

Credit Cards and Traveler's Checks:

- Major Credit Cards: Widely accepted in most hotels, restaurants, and larger shops. Visa and Mastercard are the most commonly accepted brands. Small, local businesses might prefer cash.
- Traveler's Checks: While less common these days, traveler's checks can still be used in some banks and currency exchange offices. However, their acceptance is declining, so relying primarily on cash, credit cards, or ATM withdrawals is recommended.

Important Tips:

Carry a Small Amount of Euros: Having some Euros on hand upon arrival is helpful for taxis, airport purchases, or small street vendors who might not accept credit cards.

Inform Your Bank: Before your trip, inform your bank about your travel dates and destination to avoid having your cards blocked for suspicious activity.

Shop Around for Rates: If exchanging currency, compare rates at different banks or exchange offices before finalizing the transaction.

Consider Travel Insurance: Travel insurance can provide peace of mind in case of lost or stolen cards or unexpected medical situations.

By following these tips and understanding Guadeloupe's currency system, you'll be well-equipped to manage your finances during your island adventure!

Health and Safety Tips

Guadeloupe is a paradise waiting to be explored, but a little preparation goes a long way in ensuring a healthy and safe vacation. Imagine basking on pristine beaches without a sunburn, exploring lush rainforests without encountering pesky mosquitos, and enjoying delicious local cuisine without any unwanted stomach troubles. Here are some essential health and safety tips to keep in mind:

Sun Safety:

- Pack Sunscreen: The Caribbean sun is strong! Don't forget about your lips and ears – sunburn in these areas is no fun.
- Seek Shade: Plan your activities around the sun's peak intensity (typically between 11:00 AM and 3:00 PM) and seek shade during these hours. Relax under an umbrella on the beach, explore museums or historical sites, or simply take a siesta!
- Stay Hydrated: The hot, humid climate can lead to dehydration quickly. Avoid sugary drinks and opt for water or fresh coconut water.

Mosquitoes and Insects:

- Insect Repellent: Pack a DEET-based insect repellent to ward off mosquitoes, especially during rainy seasons. Mosquitoes can carry diseases like Dengue fever, so prevention is key.
- Wear Light, Long Clothing: Consider wearing long, loose-fitting clothing made from breathable fabrics in the evenings, when mosquitoes are most active.

Food and Water Safety:

- Stick to Bottled Water: Tap water in Guadeloupe is generally safe for showering and brushing teeth, but bottled water is recommended for drinking to avoid any potential stomach upset.

- Choose Wisely: Opt for freshly cooked meals at reputable restaurants. Be cautious of street vendors, especially when it comes to raw or undercooked seafood. When in doubt, leave it out!
- Wash Your Produce: If you're eating fresh fruits or vegetables, wash them thoroughly with clean water before consuming them.

General Safety:

- Be Sun-Smart: Sunglasses and a hat are essential to protect your eyes and head from the sun's harsh rays. Consider wearing water shoes when exploring rocky coastlines or coral reefs.
- Respect the Locals: Dress modestly when visiting religious sites and be respectful of local customs and traditions. A friendly smile and a "bonjour" (hello) go a long way!
- Secure Your Belongings: Petty theft can occur anywhere, so keep an eye on your belongings, especially in crowded areas.
- Emergency Numbers: Store emergency contact information in your phone, including the local police number (17) and ambulance number (15).

Medical Care:

- Travel Insurance: Consider purchasing travel insurance, especially if you have any pre-existing medical conditions.
- Pharmacies: Pharmacies (pharmacies) are readily available throughout Guadeloupe and offer basic over-the-counter medications.
- By following these simple tips, you can ensure a healthy and safe vacation in Guadeloupe, allowing you to focus on creating lasting memories in this captivating island paradise!

Communication (Internet and Mobile Networks)

Staying connected in Guadeloupe is a breeze! Imagine sharing breathtaking vacation photos with loved ones back home, checking emails for important updates, or using navigation apps to explore hidden gems – all with a reliable internet connection. Here's what you need to know about staying connected on your island adventure:

Mobile Network Providers:

Multiple Options: Several mobile network providers operate in Guadeloupe, including Orange Caraïbes, SFR Caraïbe Mobile, Digicel, and Free Mobile. Choosing the best option depends on your needs and budget.

Before You Go:

Contact Your Provider: Contact your current mobile provider to inquire about international roaming options and potential charges. Some providers offer special travel packages, while others might charge hefty fees for data usage abroad.

Purchasing a Local SIM Card:

Convenience and Cost-Effectiveness: Consider purchasing a local SIM card upon arrival in Guadeloupe. This can often be more cost-effective than relying solely on international roaming charges.

Where to Buy: SIM cards are readily available at mobile phone stores, convenience stores (like Carrefour Market), and airport kiosks. Look for prepaid SIM card options advertised as "sans engagement" (without commitment).

Popular Mobile Network Providers:

Orange Caraïbes: Offers good island-wide coverage and various prepaid data plans.

Digicel: Another strong contender, known for competitive rates and good coverage.

Staying Online:

Free Wi-Fi: Many hotels, restaurants, cafes, and public spaces offer free Wi-Fi access. Connection speeds and reliability can vary, but it's a convenient option for basic browsing and messaging.

Mobile Data: Using your local SIM card with a data plan provides more flexibility and allows you to stay connected on the go. Data plans can be purchased in various denominations, depending on your data usage needs.

Important Tips:

- Unlock Your Phone: Ensure your phone is unlocked to work with different SIM cards. Contact your current provider for unlocking instructions if needed.
- Check Data Usage: Monitor your data usage to avoid exceeding your plan's limit and incurring additional charges. Most providers offer apps or online portals to track your usage.
- Alternative Options: Consider portable Wi-Fi hotspots as an alternative, especially if you're traveling with a group or require a more consistent connection. These can be rented in advance or upon arrival in Guadeloupe.

By following these tips and choosing the right communication options, you'll ensure you stay connected and can share your Guadeloupean adventure with the world!

CHAPTER 8. Accommodation

Guadeloupe offers a diverse range of accommodation options to suit every taste and budget. Imagine waking up to ocean views in a luxurious hotel, experiencing local charm in a cozy guesthouse, or enjoying the privacy and space of a private villa. Here's a breakdown of three popular choices to help you find your perfect Guadeloupean nest:

Types of Accommodation (Hotels, Guesthouses, Villas)

1. Hotels: Comfort and Convenience

Hotels in Guadeloupe cater to a variety of travelers, from budget-conscious backpackers to luxury-seeking vacationers.

Auberge de la Vieille Tour (Gosier): This charming hotel in Gosier offers a delightful blend of French and Creole architecture, comfortable rooms, and a delightful on-site restaurant. Perfect for those seeking a comfortable stay with a touch of local flavor. (Price range: Moderate)

Caravelle Beach Resort (Sainte-Anne): Located directly on the stunning Caravelle Beach, this resort offers spacious rooms, multiple pools, and various water sports activities. Ideal for families seeking a fun-filled beachfront vacation. (Price range: High)

2. Guesthouses: A Taste of Local Charm

Guesthouses (gîtes) offer a unique opportunity to experience Guadeloupean hospitality and culture firsthand. Imagine staying in a charming Creole-style house, enjoying personalized attention from local hosts, and potentially interacting with fellow travelers.

Chez Maguy (Deshaies): This family-run guesthouse in Deshaies offers comfortable rooms, a beautiful garden setting, and delicious homemade breakfasts. The owners are a wealth of local knowledge and can recommend hidden gems to explore. (Price range: Budget-friendly)

La Douceur de Vivre (Sainte-Rose): Nestled in the hills of Sainte-Rose, this guesthouse provides a tranquil retreat with panoramic views. Guests can enjoy a refreshing pool, unwind on the sun terrace, and savor homemade meals prepared with local ingredients. (Price range: Moderate)

3. Villas: Privacy and Space

Villas offer the ultimate privacy and space, perfect for groups or families seeking a home away from home. Imagine relaxing in your private pool, enjoying barbecues on the terrace, and having the flexibility to come and go as you please.

Villa Bleu Caraïbes (Trois-Îlets): Located on the southern tip of Basse-Terre, this luxurious villa boasts stunning ocean views, a private pool, and spacious living areas. Ideal for a luxurious getaway with stunning scenery. (Price range: High)

Ti Kaz Fleurs (Bouillante): This charming Creole-style villa in Bouillante offers comfortable accommodations, a private plunge pool, and a delightful garden setting. Perfect for those seeking a taste of local charm with added privacy. (Price range: Moderate)

Finding Your Perfect Place:

Research online platforms like booking websites or travel agent resources to explore various options and compare prices.

Consider your location preferences (beachfront, quiet village, etc.) and desired amenities (pool, on-site dining, etc.).

Read guest reviews to get insights into other travelers' experiences.

Contact accommodation providers directly to inquire about specific rates and availability, especially during peak season.

With so many captivating options to choose from, you're sure to find the perfect accommodation to make your Guadeloupean adventure unforgettable!

Recommended Places to Stay

Guadeloupe's charm extends beyond its stunning landscapes and captivating culture. Imagine discovering hidden gems – charming boutique hotels brimming with local character, intimate eco-lodges nestled amidst lush rainforests, or beachfront bungalows offering an unparalleled connection to the ocean. Here are a few unique escapes to consider for your Guadeloupean adventure:

Boutique Bliss:

Hotel Auberge de la Mare (Pointe-à-Pitre): Step back in time at this beautifully restored colonial mansion in Pointe-à-Pitre. This intimate hotel offers tastefully decorated rooms, a refreshing pool courtyard, and a delightful on-site restaurant serving Creole specialties. Mingle with fellow travelers in the elegant lounge or explore the nearby city streets. (Price range: Moderate)

Eco-Friendly Adventures:

Ecolodge Sukali (Bouillante): Immerse yourself in nature at Ecolodge Sukali, nestled in the heart of the Bouillante rainforest. These comfortable bungalows offer stunning views of the surrounding landscape, while eco-friendly practices minimize environmental impact. Explore hidden waterfalls, hike through lush trails, and reconnect with nature. (Price range: Moderate)

Beachfront Paradise:

Les Filaos (Deshaies): Wake up to the sound of waves lapping at your doorstep at Les Filaos, a collection of charming bungalows directly on Deshaies Bay. Imagine stepping out onto your private terrace, breathing in the fresh ocean air, and enjoying breathtaking sunrises over the turquoise waters. Kayaks and paddleboards are available for exploring the coastline, while the lively village of Deshaies is just a short stroll away. (Price range: Budget-friendly to Moderate)

Off-the-Beaten-Path Retreat:

Habitation La Coulisse (Sainte-Rose): Escape the crowds and discover tranquility at Habitation La Coulisse, a restored 18th-century plantation house nestled in the hills of Sainte-Rose. This charming property offers spacious rooms, a refreshing pool, and breathtaking panoramic views. Explore the surrounding gardens brimming with tropical flora and fauna, or simply relax on the sun terrace and soak in the serenity. (Price range: Moderate)

Remember:

When considering these recommendations, keep in mind that prices can fluctuate depending on the season and availability.

It's always best to contact the properties directly for the most accurate rates and booking information.

Embrace the spirit of discovery and find your unique Guadeloupean escape! These hidden gems promise an unforgettable experience that goes beyond the ordinary hotel stay.

CHAPTER 9. Shopping and Souvenirs

Guadeloupe isn't just a visual feast; it's a shopper's paradise! Imagine bustling markets overflowing with colorful spices and handcrafted souvenirs, charming streets lined with unique boutiques, and air-conditioned malls housing international brands. Here's a glimpse into Guadeloupe's shopping scene to help you discover the perfect treasures:

Markets and Shopping Districts

Immerse Yourself in Local Life at the Markets:

- Marché Saint-Antoine (Pointe-à-Pitre): This historic market in Pointe-à-Pitre is a sensory overload in the best way possible! Weave through stalls overflowing with fresh produce, fragrant spices like cinnamon and nutmeg, and an array of local crafts. Be prepared to bargain for the best prices and soak up the vibrant atmosphere. (Open Monday to Saturday, 6:00 AM to 3:00 PM)
- Marché de Basse-Terre: Located in the heart of Basse-Terre, this bustling market offers a glimpse into the island's agricultural bounty. Stalls overflow with fresh fruits and vegetables, local

honey, and colorful flowers. Don't forget to sample some of the delicious local snacks like accras (fritters) or savory samosas. (Open Monday to Saturday, 6:00 AM to 3:00 PM)

Explore Quaint Boutiques and Local Crafts:

- Durance (Pointe-à-Pitre): Indulge in the fragrant world of Durance, a French chain offering a delightful selection of soaps, lotions, and home fragrances made with natural ingredients. Imagine finding the perfect souvenir – a tropical-scented candle or a luxurious body lotion infused with local flora. (Several locations throughout Guadeloupe, with varying opening times)
- Village artisanal de Sainte-Anne (Sainte-Anne): Located in the heart of Sainte-Anne, this charming village is a haven for handcrafted souvenirs. Imagine browsing through stalls brimming with colorful madras scarves, hand-painted pottery, and intricate straw baskets. Interact with local artisans, learn about their techniques, and find unique treasures to take home. (Open daily, with varying hours for individual shops)

For the Modern Shopper:

Centre Saint-John Perse (Pointe-à-Pitre): This modern shopping center offers a mix of international brands and local stores. Imagine browsing through trendy clothing stores, finding the perfect pair of sunglasses for the beach, or grabbing a coffee break at a chic cafe. (Open every day, with extended hours during weekends)

Beyond the Shopping Bag:

- Remember: Cash is still widely accepted, especially at local markets and smaller shops, but credit cards are becoming increasingly common.
- Haggling: Don't be afraid to bargain at local markets, particularly for handcrafted items. It's all part of the experience!
- Opening Times: Most shops adhere to standard business hours, typically Monday to Saturday from 9:00 AM to 5:00 PM, with some staying open later on weekdays. Many shops close on Sundays.

Embrace the spirit of discovery and embark on a shopping adventure in Guadeloupe! From bustling markets and charming villages to modern malls, you're sure to find unique treasures to bring home a piece of this captivating island paradise.

Unique Souvenirs to Buy

Guadeloupe's charm extends beyond its stunning beaches and vibrant culture. Dive into the island's soul by bringing home a one-of-a-kind souvenir that tells a story. Here are some unique finds to commemorate your Guadeloupean adventure:

A Taste of the Islands:

Rhum arrangé (Spiced Rum): This quintessential Guadeloupean beverage is a must-have. Imagine bottles bursting with colorful fruits, spices, and local rum, creating an explosion of flavor. Choose from classic flavors like vanilla or pineapple, or opt for something more adventurous like chili or coffee. Find them at most supermarkets, liquor stores, or directly from local producers. (Prices vary depending on size and brand)

Madras Scarves: These colorful, lightweight cotton scarves are a symbol of Guadeloupean identity. Imagine vibrant geometric patterns or floral prints adorning everything from beach cover-ups to stylish accessories. Find them at local markets, boutiques, and street vendors. (

Local Craftsmanship:

La poterie de Sainte-Rose (Sainte-Rose Pottery): Bring home a piece of Guadeloupean artistry with handcrafted pottery from Sainte-Rose. Imagine beautifully glazed bowls, intricate vases, or decorative tiles, each piece showcasing traditional techniques passed down through generations. Visit local artisans' studios in Sainte-Rose or find their work at select boutiques.

Vannerie (Basket Weaving): Guadeloupean basket weaving is a time-honored tradition. Imagine intricate baskets crafted from natural fibers like raffia or coconut palm, perfect for storing souvenirs or adding a touch of island charm to your home. Look for them at local markets, craft villages, or directly from artisans. (Prices vary depending on size and intricacy)

A Touch of the Sea:

Colliers de coquillages (Seashell Necklaces): Embrace the island's connection to the ocean with a beautiful seashell necklace. Imagine delicate necklaces crafted from colorful shells, each piece a unique reminder of your tropical paradise. Find them at local markets, street vendors selling beach trinkets or souvenir shops.

Huile de coco (Coconut Oil): This versatile product is a natural beauty secret and a delicious addition to your kitchen. Imagine bottles of pure, cold-pressed coconut oil, perfect for nourishing your skin or adding a tropical twist to your cooking. Find them at local markets, supermarkets, and shops specializing in natural products. (Prices vary depending on size and brand)

Beyond the Souvenir Stand:

Support Local Artisans: Many souvenirs are handcrafted by local artisans. By purchasing directly from them, you're not only getting a unique piece but also supporting the island's creative community.

Haggling: Don't be afraid to negotiate prices, especially at local markets. It's part of the cultural experience!

Packing Tips: Pack your souvenirs carefully, especially fragile items like pottery or seashell jewelry. Consider using bubble wrap or purchasing sturdy packing materials at your destination.

Let your souvenirs be more than just trinkets. Let them be conversation starters, reminding you of the sights, smells, and warmth of your unforgettable Guadeloupean adventure!

CHAPTER 10. Additional Tips and Resources

Planning a trip to Guadeloupe is exciting! But with so much to see and do, a little extra guidance can go a long way. Here's a curated list of travel agencies, websites, and apps to help you craft an unforgettable itinerary and unlock the island's hidden gems:

Travel Agencies and Tour Operators:

- Karulodge (Sainte-Anne): This local agency specializes in crafting personalized tours and excursions for all interests, from exploring hidden waterfalls and rainforests to discovering the island's rich cultural heritage. Their multilingual guides ensure a seamless experience.
- Archipel Guadeloupe (Pointe-à-Pitre): This reputable agency offers a variety of pre-designed tours, including catamaran cruises, island hopping adventures, and cultural immersion experiences. They also assist with car rentals and activity bookings. Browse their website or visit their office in Pointe-à-Pitre for details.

Useful Apps:.

Trace (app): This free app is your one-stop shop for exploring Guadeloupe's vibrant music scene. Discover upcoming concerts, find local bars and restaurants with live music performances, and immerse yourself in the island's pulsating rhythms.

Additional Tips:

- Consider Local Guides: Hiring a local guide can unlock hidden gems and provide valuable insights into Guadeloupean culture and history. Many guides are multilingual and passionate about sharing their island home.
- Learn a Few Creole Phrases: While French is the official language, a few basic Creole greetings or expressions will be greatly appreciated by locals and enhance your cultural connection.
- Download Offline Maps: Guadeloupe's internet connectivity can be spotty in remote areas. Download offline maps on your phone to ensure you never get lost while exploring the island.
- Embrace the Unexpected: Leave some room for spontaneity on your trip. Detour down a charming side street, strike up a conversation with a local or explore an unexpected beach cove. Sometimes the most memorable experiences are unplanned!

By utilizing these resources and embracing a spirit of adventure, you'll be well on your way to crafting a truly unforgettable Guadeloupean experience. Bon voyage!

Language and Cultural Etiquette

Guadeloupe's vibrant culture is a delightful blend of French and Creole influences. While French is the official language, Creole is widely spoken in everyday life. Here's a helpful guide to navigating the language barrier and embracing local customs:

Common Phrases (French and Creole)

Common Phrases (French & Creole):

French | Creole | English

-------- | -------- | --------

Bonjour | Bonjou | Hello

Bonsoir | Bonswa | Good evening

Merci | Mèsi | Thank you

S'il vous plaît | Sè-voud-plé | Please

Excusez-moi | Ekzize mwen | Excuse me

Oui | Wi | Yes

Non | Non | No

Parlez-vous anglais? | Ès-u ou ka palé anglais? | Do you speak English?

Je ne comprends pas | Mwen pa ka konprann | I don't understand

Cultural Tips for Travelers

Cultural Tips for Travelers:

A Few Words Go a Long Way: Even a few basic French or Creole phrases will be greatly appreciated by locals. A simple "bonjour" when entering a shop or "merci" after receiving service shows respect and effort.

- Embrace the Smile: Guadeloupeans are known for their friendly and welcoming nature. A warm smile goes a long way in establishing a connection and overcoming any language barriers.
- Respect Personal Space: Guadeloupeans tend to maintain a slightly closer physical distance than people in some cultures. Be mindful of this and avoid standing too close in conversations.

- Dress Modestly for Religious Sites: When visiting churches or other religious sites, dress modestly with shoulders and knees covered.
- Tipping: Tipping is not customary in Guadeloupe, but a small gratuity (around 10%) is always appreciated for exceptional service at restaurants.
- Respect the Rhythm of Life: Life in Guadeloupe moves at a slower pace than in some Western countries. Embrace the relaxed atmosphere, be patient when waiting for service, and enjoy the laid-back island vibe.
- Bargaining: Haggling is expected at local markets and with street vendors. Do so politely and with a smile, and be prepared to walk away if you can't reach an agreement.
- Photography Etiquette: Always ask permission before taking photos of people, especially locals going about their daily lives."Ès sé mwen ké pran yon poto?" (Creole) shows respect for privacy.

Remember: A little cultural awareness goes a long way in enriching your Guadeloupean experience. By making an effort to learn a few basic phrases and respecting local customs, you'll be warmly welcomed and gain a deeper appreciation for the island's unique charm.

CHAPTER 11. Sample Itineraries

Guadeloupe's allure extends beyond its stunning beaches. Imagine immersing yourself in lush rainforests, exploring charming villages, and uncovering the island's rich culture. This one-week itinerary offers a taste of everything Guadeloupe has to offer:

One-Week Itinerary

Day 1: Pointe-à-Pitre & Basse-Terre Bliss

- Morning: Start your adventure in Pointe-à-Pitre, the vibrant capital city. Explore the bustling Marché Saint-Antoine (open Monday-Saturday, 6:00 AM to 3:00 PM), indulge in a delicious breakfast at a local cafe, and soak up the lively atmosphere.
- Afternoon: Take a scenic ferry ride across to Basse-Terre, the island's dramatic western counterpart. Check in to your hotel in Deshaies, a charming village nestled along a beautiful bay. Take a stroll along the shore or go snorkeling in the pristine waters throughout the afternoon.

Day 2: Rainforest Rendezvous & Cultural Immersion

- Morning: Embark on a guided hike through the heart of Guadeloupe National Park. Explore the lush rainforest trails, marvel at cascading waterfalls like Chutes de Carbet, and keep an eye out for colorful birds and exotic flora. Park entrance fees vary depending on the chosen trail.
- Afternoon: Head to the charming village of Sainte-Rose. Visit the Habitation La Coulisse (admission fees apply, opening times vary), a restored 18th-century plantation house, to learn about the island's colonial history. Take a stroll through the lovely grounds and take in the expansive vistas.

Day 3: Island Hopping & Marine Majesty

- Full Day: Join a catamaran cruise to explore the surrounding islands like Les Saintes or Marie-Galante. Imagine snorkeling in vibrant coral reefs, sunbathing on pristine beaches, and indulging in a delicious onboard lunch. Prices and departure times vary depending on the chosen tour operator.

Day 4: Grande-Terre Delights & Beachside Bliss

- Morning: Travel to Grande-Terre, the island's eastern counterpart, known for its white-sand beaches and calm turquoise waters. Check-in at your hotel in Saint-François, a popular resort town offering various amenities.

- Afternoon: Spend the afternoon soaking up the sun on the idyllic Plage de la Caravelle. Go for a swim, try your hand at kayaking or paddleboarding, or simply relax under the shade of palm trees.

Day 5: Pointe des Châteaux & Historical Gems

- Morning: Explore the dramatic Pointe des Châteaux, a peninsula on the eastern tip of Grande-Terre. Hike along rugged cliffs, marvel at the unique rock formations sculpted by wind and waves and enjoy breathtaking ocean views.
- Afternoon: Head to the historic town of Le Moule, known for its 17th-century Fort Louis Delgrès (entrance fees apply, open daily except Tuesdays). Learn about Guadeloupe's colonial past and explore the well-preserved fortifications.

Day 6: Foodie Frenzy & Local Flavors

- Morning: Spend the morning exploring the bustling market in Saint-Anne (open Monday-Saturday, 6:00 AM to 3:00 PM). Sample exotic fruits, indulge in local delicacies like accras (fritters), and browse handcrafted souvenirs.

- Afternoon: Take a cooking class and learn the secrets of traditional Guadeloupean cuisine. Prepare a delicious meal with fresh, local ingredients and enjoy the fruits of your labor in a convivial atmosphere. Prices and booking details vary depending on the chosen provider.

Day 7: Relaxation & Reflection

- Full Day: Spend your last day basking in the beauty of Guadeloupe. Relax on the beach, read a book under a palm tree, or simply reflect on the unforgettable memories you've created. Enjoy a farewell dinner at a beachfront restaurant, savoring the island's delicious seafood and breathtaking sunsets.

Remember: This itinerary is just a suggestion. Feel free to adjust it based on your interests and pace. Guadeloupe offers something for everyone, so embrace the spirit of discovery and create your unforgettable adventure!

Family-Friendly Trip

Guadeloupe isn't just a romantic paradise; it's a haven for families seeking adventure, relaxation, and cultural immersion. Imagine splashing in crystal-clear waters, exploring hidden waterfalls, and creating memories that will last a lifetime. This one-week itinerary caters to families with children of all ages:

Day 1: Pointe-à-Pitre & Grande-Terre Greetings

- Morning: Arrive in Pointe-à-Pitre, the bustling capital city. Enjoy a delicious breakfast at a family-friendly café, allowing everyone to adjust to the island time zone. Consider visiting the aquarium (admission fees apply, open daily) for a glimpse into the underwater world of the Caribbean.
- Afternoon: Take a taxi or pre-arranged shuttle to your accommodation on Grande-Terre, the eastern island known for its calm beaches. Check-in and spend the afternoon unwinding on the white sand of Plage de la Caravelle, perfect for building sandcastles and splashing in the gentle waves.

Day 2: Splashing Fun & Animal Encounters

- Morning: Head to Aqualand Guadeloupe, a water park offering thrilling slides, lazy rivers, and a dedicated children's area. Let the whole family enjoy a day filled with laughter and refreshing water fun.
- Afternoon: Drive to Parc Zoologique de Guadeloupe (admission fees apply, open daily) in

Basse-Terre. Explore the diverse animal life of the Caribbean, from playful monkeys to colorful parrots. Kids will be mesmerized by the vibrant flora and fauna.

Day 3: Rainforest Ramble & Waterfall Wonders

- Morning: Embark on a guided hike (suitable for families) through a portion of Guadeloupe National Park. Explore the lush rainforest, marvel at cascading waterfalls like Saut de la Lézarde, and keep an eye out for colorful butterflies and exotic birds. Park entrance fees vary depending on the chosen trail.
- Afternoon: Relax on the black sand beach of Plage de Grande Anse after your hike. The calm waters are perfect for swimming, and the unique volcanic sand adds an exciting touch. Enjoy a picnic lunch under the shade of palm trees.

Day 4: Island Hopping & Marine Majesty

- Full Day: Join a family-friendly catamaran cruise to explore the surrounding islands like Les Saintes. Imagine snorkeling in vibrant coral reefs teeming with colorful fish, enjoying a delicious onboard lunch, and participating in fun games and activities designed for all ages. Prices and departure times vary depending on the chosen tour operator.

Day 5: Historical Exploration & Cultural Delights

- Morning: Travel to Basse-Terre and visit the charming town of Sainte-Rose. Explore the interactive exhibits at the Musée Costumes et Traditions (admission fees apply, open Tuesday-Sunday) to learn about Guadeloupean history and traditional clothing.
- Afternoon: Head to the bustling market in Basse-Terre (open Monday-Saturday, 6:00 AM to 3:00 PM). Let the kids experience the sights, sounds, and smells of a local market. Sample exotic fruits, grab some fresh snacks, and browse for unique souvenirs.

Day 6: Beach Bliss & Local Flavors

- Morning: Spend the morning soaking up the sun on the pristine Plage de la Perle. The calm turquoise waters and gentle waves are ideal for families with young children. Enjoy building sandcastles, renting paddle boards for a fun exploration, or simply relaxing under the shade of umbrellas.
- Afternoon: Take a cooking class designed for families and learn the secrets of preparing a

traditional Guadeloupean dish like Colombo (a flavorful curry). This interactive experience allows everyone to participate in the fun and enjoy the delicious creations afterward. Prices and booking details vary depending on the chosen provider.

Day 7: Relaxation & Reflection

- Full Day: Spend your last day creating lasting memories. Relax on the beach, revisit a favorite spot, or simply enjoy a leisurely breakfast overlooking the turquoise waters. In the evening, enjoy a farewell family dinner at a beachfront restaurant, reminiscing about your unforgettable Guadeloupean adventure.

Remember: This itinerary is just a suggestion. Feel free to adjust it based on your family's interests and pace. Consider incorporating activities like kayaking, exploring hidden beaches, or attending a local cultural event. Guadeloupe offers endless possibilities for family fun, so embrace the spirit of adventure and create a memorable island escape together!

Adventure Travel Plan

Guadeloupe isn't just a beach paradise; it's a playground for adrenaline junkies and nature enthusiasts. Imagine scaling volcanic peaks, kayaking through hidden mangroves, and exploring the underwater world teeming with colorful life. This one-week itinerary caters to thrill-seekers and outdoor adventurers:

Day 1: Pointe-à-Pitre & Gearing Up

- Morning: Arrive in Pointe-à-Pitre, the bustling capital city. Fuel up with a delicious breakfast at a local cafe and explore the shops for any last-minute adventure gear. Consider visiting a reputable tour operator to book guided excursions for the upcoming days.
- Afternoon: Take a ferry or pre-arranged shuttle to Basse-Terre, the dramatic western island renowned for its natural beauty. Check in to your accommodation in Deshaies, a charming village nestled near stunning beaches. Spend the afternoon relaxing on the beach or enjoying a refreshing swim.

Day 2: Conquering La Soufrière & Geothermal Wonders

- Early Morning: Embark on a challenging but rewarding guided hike to the summit of La Soufrière volcano. Hike through lush rainforest trails, marvel at the otherworldly volcanic landscape, and witness breathtaking panoramic views. Early departure is recommended due to heat and afternoon cloud cover. Park entrance fees and guide fees apply.
- Afternoon: Relax and soothe your muscles at the natural hot springs near Bouillante. Imagine soaking in the warm, mineral-rich waters surrounded by lush vegetation. Entrance fees may apply depending on the chosen location.

Day 3: Kayaking Adventure & Mangrove Exploration

- Morning: Join a guided kayaking tour through the intricate maze of the Grand Cul-de-Sac Marin nature reserve. Paddle through tranquil mangrove forests, teeming with birdlife, and discover hidden coves and idyllic beaches inaccessible by land. Tour prices and departure times vary depending on the chosen operator.
- Afternoon: Spend the afternoon snorkeling or diving on the Jacques Cousteau Underwater Reserve (reserve fees apply). Explore vibrant coral reefs, encounter a kaleidoscope of fish, and witness shipwrecks teeming with marine life.

Day 4: Canyoning Challenge & Hidden Waterfalls

- Full Day: Embark on an exhilarating canyoning adventure with a certified guide. Rappel down cascading waterfalls, swim in crystal-clear pools, and explore hidden canyons carved by nature. Canyoneering tours require good physical fitness and swimming ability. Prices and booking details vary depending on the chosen operator.

Day 5: Island Hopping & Cliff Jumping

- Full Day: Join a day trip to the rugged island of La Désirade, known for its dramatic cliffs and secluded beaches. Hike to the island's highest point for breathtaking views, and enjoy a thrilling cliff-jumping experience into crystal-clear waters (with proper guidance). Tour prices and departure times vary depending on the chosen operator.

Day 6: Mountain Biking & Scenic Trails

- Morning: Rent mountain bikes and explore the scenic trails of Basse-Terre National Park. Traverse rolling hills, conquer challenging climbs, and enjoy breathtaking vistas of the lush rainforest and the turquoise coastline. Bike rental shops are available in Deshaies and other towns.

- Afternoon: Relax on the Plage de Grande Anse, a black sand beach with powerful waves perfect for experienced surfers. Alternatively, rent stand-up paddleboards and explore the calm waters along the coast.

Day 7: Relaxation & Reflection

- Full Day: Spend your last day unwinding and reminiscing about your thrilling adventures. Catch some rays on the beach, indulge in a massage at a spa, or simply relax with a good book overlooking the ocean. Enjoy a farewell dinner at a beachfront restaurant, savoring the delicious cuisine and the unforgettable memories of your Guadeloupean adventure.

Remember: This itinerary is a suggestion. Feel free to adjust it based on your experience level, desired activities, and risk tolerance. Guadeloupe offers countless opportunities for adventure; embrace the challenge and discover the island's hidden gems!

CHAPTER 12. Maps of Guadeloupe

Maps is your go-to app on your computer for global navigation. You may use it to search for locations, receive instructions for walking, bicycling, or driving, and even browse reviews and images. The interesting black-and-white squares known as QR codes have the ability to record location data. You can instantly be transported to a certain location on Google Maps by using the camera on your phone to scan a QR code—no typing needed!

GUADELOUPE

LES JARDINS
DE ZEPHYR

SCAN THE QR CODE

1. Open your device's camera app.
2. Point the camera at the Qi code.
3. Ensure the OR cede is within the frame and well-ut.
4. Wait for your device to recognize the OR code.
5. Once recognized, tap on the notification or follow the prompt to access the content or action associated with the OR code

Basse-Terre

SCAN THE QR CODE

1. Open your device's camera app.
2. Point the camera at the Qi code.
3. Ensure the OR cede is within the frame and well-ut.
4. Wait for your device to recognize the OR code.
5. Once recognized, tap on the notification or follow the prompt to access the content or action associated with the OR code

Grande-Terre

SCAN THE QR CODE

1. Open your device's camera app.
2. Point the camera at the Qi code.
3. Ensure the OR cede is within the frame and well-ut.
4. Wait for your device to recognize the OR code.
5. Once recognized, tap on the notification or follow the prompt to access the content or action associated with the OR code

Guadeloupe National Park (Basse-Terre)

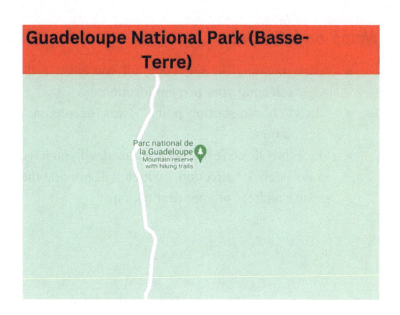

SCAN THE QR CODE

1. Open your device's camera app.
2. Point the camera at the Qi code.
3. Ensure the OR cede is within the frame and well-ut.
4. Wait for your device to recognize the OR code.
5. Once recognized, tap on the notification or follow the prompt to access the content or action associated with the OR code

Maps and Guides

- After scanning the QR code, all you have to do After selecting your present location,
- Click "choose starting point." Next, decide on a "destination."
- Once the QR code has been scanned, all you have to do is click "direction," which will provide the precise address of your destination.

Conclusion

Guadeloupe isn't just a destination; it's an experience that lingers long after you depart. Imagine the warmth of the sun on your skin, the rhythm of the waves lapping at the shore, and the vibrant tapestry of sights, sounds, and flavors that have filled your senses. As you pack your bags and prepare to say goodbye, here's a hope that these memories become cherished treasures:

Beyond the Beach: Guadeloupe's charm extends far beyond its pristine beaches. You've likely explored lush rainforests, climbed volcanic peaks, and kayaked through hidden mangroves, uncovering the island's diverse landscapes and rich biodiversity.

A Cultural Tapestry: Guadeloupe's cultural tapestry is a beautiful blend of French and Creole influences. You may have savored the flavors of local cuisine, learned a few basic Creole phrases, or even danced to the pulsating rhythms of live music, gaining a deeper appreciation for the island's unique heritage.

Warm Encounters: The Guadeloupean people are renowned for their friendly and welcoming nature. You've likely experienced their genuine smiles, helpful gestures, and infectious joie de vivre, making you feel like a cherished guest rather than just a tourist.

As you depart, take a piece of Guadeloupe with you. It could be a handcrafted souvenir, a bag of freshly roasted coffee beans, or simply the unforgettable memories etched in your heart. Guadeloupe beckons you to return, discover new hidden gems, and revisit cherished experiences. Until next time, au revoir, Guadeloupe!

Made in the USA
Las Vegas, NV
13 July 2024

92273071R00069